The Correlation

Oscar Matongo

ISBN: 978-1-77925-995-0

DEDICATION

This paper is dedicated to my fellow Zimbabweans

CONTENTS

Acknowledgments   v

1   Preface   vi

2   Polity and Politics: An Overview   1

3   Correlation of Politics and Economy   21

4   Inquisitive for a New Routine   49

5   Balancing Act Concept   61

6   Conclusion   77

7   Reference List   78

ACKNOWLEDGMENTS

A great appreciation to Tinotenda Melissa Mamvoto and Tapiwa Dondo for stupefying support. I would like to thank my mother Theresa, my brother Garikai for huge motivations, and above all praise and thankful to the Superior Deity.

PREFACE

In a society with social unrest, trepidation, perplexity, and economic meltdown, what is a panacea required to restore social and economic order? This is the fundamental question that could and would stimulate the mind of individuals to think about feasible solutions to end privation, worry, and discomfit state among the citizens. The driving tool for economic revival and transformation is stable politics. Stable politics give room for attainment of social solidarity, oneness, common interest for the common good, and a harmonious polity. All these stand as remedies to the incessant economic recession. This paper intends to verify the alternative hypothesis that the incessant economic recession that Zimbabwe experiences has a close correlation with distorted or unstable politics. In other words, the economic challenges that affect the nation correlate with the political conditions of the day. This verdict is presented as an irrefutable claim in this paper and its well-meaning can be justified by probabilistic. The conceptualization part enthuse the critical areas that mold Zimbabwean politics in a point and solution presentation. In this book, the chapter on the correlation of politics and economy is characterized by an ebb and flow economic trend from 2004 up to 2018 as it was heralded by political environment. The trend typifies an oscillation of economic trend that depicts up and down pattern a teeter-totter system eventuated by a strong determinant factor of distorted or unstable politics. The correlation of politics and economy incisively denotes how the ossification of unstable or distorted political system influenced the oscillation of economic graph leading to inveterate ebb and flow. Unity among political institutions is a praiseworthy modus operandi. The ipso facto presented as a miraculous modus vivendi that leaves an indelible era of 2009 to 2013. The inquisitive for a new routine chapter intends to encapsulate the way in which citizens can be freed from the invidious position through the introduction of fundamental political reforms. Finally the balancing act concept is a solution forwarded in this book which can be emphasized due to its practicality. Yet, the focus here is not to describe the political environment and its consequences but to illustrate cause and effect relationship between politics and economy. In other words, unstable politics result in unstable economy and stable politics create stable economy. This book is not hundred percent sagacious piece of writing but consists of reflections concerning Zimbabwe's politics and economy which can be tackled from the analysis of the cause and effect relationship between the two. This book gives an appreciation to qualitative and quantitative research methods basing on empiricism and statistical data presentation respectively in order to vindicate the cause and effect relationship between politics and economy. The first chapter is the conceptualization of Zimbabwean politics, followed by the presentation of the correlation of politics and economy, the penultimate chapter is the inquisitive for a new routine and finally the balancing act principle.

THE POLITY AND POLITICS-AN OVERVIEW

What is behind the teetering economy?

The above question is central in this discussion of the conceptualization of Zimbabwean politics. For the quest of understanding the sluggish pace of economic development one makes politics and economy paradoxically compatible. Zimbabwean politics needs to be analyzed with a white eye ready to see justice and injustice, fairness and unfairness, repressive and progressive circumstances that together makes a true game of politics of the nation. This stands as a stepping stone on which one begins to scrutiny the odious, and glooming sides of politics of the nation that one way or the other contribute to the self-robustness of individual in evil or good doings. A general overview of Zimbabwean politics denotes that the nation is divided into two extreme sections that is the participant group and the parochial who objectively confined themselves to their model of parochialism and stay under the marginalized margin line of politics. Such an inferiority complex disgusted them and cogently distant themselves from politics, the answer to the question of minority participants in a society with majority of people who qualify to be participants in political processes and activities especially elections. From a quantitative point of view, the majority of citizens can be vividly pictured as the citizens without hope for the prosperity of the nation either geared by politics or strong economic reforms perse. As a result the majority tend to relax and stay in-doors rather than to be the sojourners or wanderers political participants. Among the citizens who distanced themselves from politics, there are some who participate in elections regularly but just for formality without an inward motif of politics.

HIERARCHICAL ARRANGEMENT AND THE BALOONING BUREAUCRACY

The politics of the nation can be discussed from social arrangement and stratification point of view. Zimbabwe as a polity is characterized by a pyramidal social arrangement that is few members from the bureaucratic class occupy the zenith part of a pyramid, minority rich middle class at the middle and the masses, the ordinary citizens at the bottom. It is widely accepted that, every nation is defined by social stratification even in those that adopt communism as the reigning ideology, the gap between the poor and rich are visibly seen. The lucrative part in those nations is that, the market forces operate in a free environment neither controlled by the rich nor poor, in the long run the strong middle class could emerge and the market forces vested on their shoulders. The middle class members do not control the market forces but they envisaged them through their activities hence, no monopolization of market forces a typical example of good governance and a path to economic boom and high level of success. The mushrooming of strong bureaucratic class which perform a monitoring function of market forces played a critical role in slowdown economy. The intervention of this class in market forces create a situation of high state intervention rather a condition of minimal state. A scenario of high state intervention and monopolization of market forces hijack the forces of economic re-construction from the exact path and directed it to the turbulent route of economic meltdown. A solution to this scenario of enormous rise of bureaucracy and fall of state potentialities to perform their activities is de-bureaucratization which pave way for laissez faire economy, a strong weapon for the reintroduction of minimal state. Adams and Dyson (2003) stress that, in the present world, human beings lack the capacity to govern themselves. How, then government should be organized so as not to be inimical to the real nature and needs of its citizens? The answer is a minimal state: a state that is as non-coercive as possible and that leaves citizens with the greatest possible degree of freedom to develop their potentialities with dignity and self-respect. The problem is that the social stratification in Zimbabwean context is deep seated and worsened by the continuous rise of bureaucracy which purport to control market forces. How then economy flourish on such situation? Remains a question which requires a great attention from the intellectuals and ordinary citizens. It is crucial to note that, buoyant economy can be attained when the market forces are freed from the hands of the bureaucratic class. The transformation of economy goes hand in hand with the transformation of society that is its arrangement in response to economic activities. Without social transformation as buoyed by the politics of the day, the nation's ability to cause economy to transmute will be curtailed. A power retardation from the bureaucratic class gives rise to self-confidence, self-robustness, self-actualization, and the restoration of self-esteem among the masses as they would receive a worth capability to stand on the ground for their own and race with each other behind the market system. The prevailing social arrangement that manifest in the sense of stupefying bureaucracy depicts a complicated scenario that weigh against economic progression.

NATIONAL GOVERNMENT AND THE POSITION OF STATE

Nothing much can be discussed in this part except the centralization of state activities at the national level. The system is a hindrance to the potentialities and capability of the local government to initiate and perform independent activities which usher in development at local level. The inferiority complex and assumed subservient position of local government to the national government incapacitate the former leading to the emergence of a critical gap that draws the attention of the latter. In the long run, it will be difficult, if not impossible for the government to run and monitor both the national and state activities. The point of limitless poverty and majority of people living under poverty datum line is a pertinent illustration of the incapacitation of local government. In the contemporary world, centralization system is more than a route left by the past, it influences the existing order but it cannot shape the future. In a polity with people without power and authority to initiate something new, while the potentialities to develop something new being taken away from them and living in a condition of adopting abstraction policies from superiors, devolution is a way forward and a preemptive way to guard against abstractionism. It is crucial to note that, devolution can be highly credited for economic revival and transformation due to the performance and effort which can be put forward for state development by the freed natives at local level. The continuation of centralization system typify a cognitive distortion of progression and regression that is a significant support for economic repression undermining prosperity.

DEGREE OF COMPLACENCY

From a superficial analysis of Zimbabwean politics, the issue of citizens agreeing with the same is another ingredient behind a recipe for distorted politics. Masunungure (2006) termed this normalizing the abnormal. The concomitant of distorted politics and economic meltdown in Zimbabwe can be attributed to the failure of citizens to be fully disquieting enough with economic quagmire so that they resort in nation building through launching a real democracy from below. Lenin (1999:16) notes that, "democracy must be built at once from below, through the initiative of the masses themselves, through the effective participation in all fields of state activity, without supervision from above, without the bureaucracy." The masses in most cases particularly in the nations that adopt democracy as a reigning political culture and embedded their policies on the fundamental rock of democratic principles are regarded as the champions who elect and set up a government, if they relax and agree with the same the nation will never prosper but remain stagnant. Then a concoction of poor governance and slowdown of economy will instantaneously develop which hampering the progress of the nation and silence citizens about Millennium Development Goals.

CITIZENS AND THE BALLOT BOX

Lack of popular participation in political activities and processes particularly elections is another striking feature of Zimbabwean politics. It is very important for all citizens to participate in elections because there is no way majority produce bad judgment. From secondary data analysis of national election records, it is shown that the number of people who engaged in regular participation in election process maintain an incessant fall from 2008 up to 2018. The analysis of voter turnout records depict that there is gradual increase in voter turnout from 2008 up to 2018. The more the number of registered voters decrease the more the number of voter turnout increases, although this might be justified in the notion that small number can be easily attended to and saved, the minority participation remains a burning issue. Table 1.1 shows the total number of registered voters and voter turnout in millions for three election years 2008, 2013, and 2018.

Table 1.1 Registered voters and voter turnout in million.

Years	Registered Voters in Million	Voter Turnout in Million
2008	5,9	2,5
2013	5,8	3,4
2018	5,5	4,8

Source: *Zimbabwe Election Commission and Zimbabwe Election Support Network Reports.*

As shown in the table 1.1 above, the number of registered voters decrease from 5,9 million in 2008 to 5,8 million in 2013, and finally to 5,5 million in 2018. The crux about these records are the gradual fall of total number of registered voters. Fig 1.1 below unravel the records in a graphical manner, showing the total number of registered voters and voter turnout in millions in respect to election years.

Fig 1.1 Registered voters and voter turnout in million.

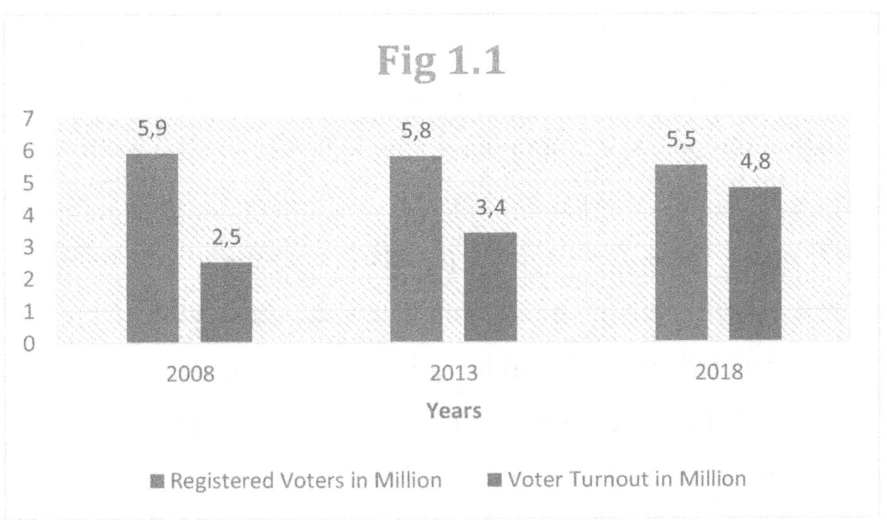

Source: *Zimbabwe Election Commission and Zimbabwe Election Support Network Reports.*

As shown in Fig 1.1, there is a gradual fall in number of registered voters and gradual increase in voter turnout from 2008 up to 2018. Approximately 3,4 million, 2,4 million and 0,7million are the differences between registered voters and voter turnout of the election years 2008, 2013, and 2018 respectively. The actual figure of people who managed to cast a ballot in 2008 was approximately 2,5 million out of around 5,9 million registered voters. Those who argued that 2008 elections recorded high percentage of citizen participation seems to commit a great error. Among the three election years 2008 recorded a least number of citizens who participated in election followed by 2013, and 2018 an exceptional record. These records point to the minority participation in a society of majority of people who qualify to vote. For instance, in 2018 there was 5,5 registered voters and 4,8 million fulfilled the voting process through casting a ballot. This depicts a minority participation of 4,8 million out of 13,061 million as per national census record of 2012 in which 59 percent constitutes an able bodied class. The 4,8 million votes out of plus 13,061 total population points to the minority participation. In 2008, the 27 June elections, the largest number of people decided otherwise although they were registered to vote, while in 2013 almost halved results was observed, and in 2018 only the few not to vote. The significant increase in voter turnout cannot be undermined but the issue of minority participants remains a burning issue. Generally the point is that election records in Zimbabwe from 2008 up to 2018 reviewed minority participation. The continuous fall in number of registered voters can be explained in the notion of citizens' action of distant themselves from politics and political activities. Election is a fundamental platform whereby citizens granted permission to elect the few representatives to rule the nation on their behalf. Although the platform comes once in a five year period, its outcome is yardstick determinant factor which influences and shapes the position of the nation for the five year period. In as much as, the nation and the regime in power adhere to the democratic tenets of citizen participation and citizen rule through the provision of an election platform from time to time, the majority of citizens undermine the opportunity and the opportunistic advantage of correcting errors, misconduct and poor governance goes unchallenged. Concisely, citizens are no longer interested in politics and political activities particularly elections. This would be an effective devastating ignorance which causes the nation to slowdown the development pace and shapes the degree of backwardness rather than to move forth through the intense contribution and tenacious grip for good judgment. The issue of citizen participation in an election cannot be treated easily by considering the political environment in general. In as much as, minority participation is a product of many factors and subject to a number of bewildering interpretations, the following reasons can be cognizant as key among others that attract real exigencies: the majority of citizens feel unrepresented in the political ladder as a result they distant themselves from politics and political activities, parochialism and hesitation to waste their votes- something should be done in order to assimilate people into a political pitch especially competitive election platforms. The correction of the mentioned reasons or factors help to abandon political upheavals since democracy will be deeply entrenched and the lustre of politics will be restored.

THE FUTURE PROGNOSIS

It is much important to provide description that intends to prefigure the future election records. The prognosis of future citizen participation in elections is in twofold that is either to maintain a status quo of gradual fall in registered voters vis-a-vis a slight increase in voter turnout or a shocking increase in the number of registered voters and the voter turnout at the same time. The reason why the future prognosis is placed in twofold is because of citizens' behavior. The study of behaviorism reviewed that human behavior is subject to change therefore, despite either predicament or conspicuous political environment human behavior is likely to change. The degree and possibility for such likelihood gives room for one to put the projection in twofold. One way or the other, citizens through their irrevocable engagement in political activities disdain the order or command from the power holders in cry for transformation in living standards. Willingly or unwillingly, adventitiously or fortuitously, the arrangement of society can be re-modified, such assiduity effort to evacuate the old system will usher in the new politics which define a new polity. The discretion then descend with full anchorage on behaviorism to prefigure the future elections record of citizens' response through participation in twofold. The continuous existing of the status quo tantamount to the incessant fall in electorate and the change significantly impacted the nature and a way in which elections would be conducted. Therefore, decrease or increase in the total number of registered voters and voter turnout are largely anchored on political environment. There is possibility that in the coming elections and beyond, the number of registered voters and voter turnout will increase or decrease depend with the political tune. For the sake of certainty, it is therefore good to prefigure the future outcomes in different political grounds. Each citizen of the nation should be assiduous for the restoration of genuine politics, a step closer to the economic revival and transformation. This can be done through the utilization of the opportunity which are regularly given to the citizens to choose an accountable leader among the alternatives. The political environment toward elections and post-election environment had a history of bearing an adverse impact on citizen disposition and minted a new character which defined by desertion of politics, staying marginalized and great acceptance to the prevailing sound with high degree of complacency. The democratic tenet of upholding the system of citizen participation is not enough, conducive election platform should be provided as a complementary trait to achieve popular participation, the two stands as eye catching features to the citizens who are no longer interested in casting a ballot. The question for the coming elections is: why the continuous fall in the number of registered voters is not as quick a subject for election contestations as the free and fair issues behind the work of the commission.

DEMONSTRATIONS AND POPULAR PROTESTS

Violent demonstrations are another outstanding area that needs to be discussed in the context of Zimbabwean politics and economy. Section 59 of the constitution postulates that, every person has a right to demonstrate and present petition, but these rights must be exercised peacefully. The point here is not to provide an explanation concerning demonstrations but to assess the hideous side of violent demonstrations orchestrated by either masses themselves, political institutions or interest groups. The starting point in this discussion is that, demonstrations in most cases went hand in hand with popular support against repressive and retrogressive actions. In this context demonstrations can be exercised to the fullest in pursuit of reversing the repressive to attain progress. The problem could arise when people starting to engage on rampage activities behind the shadow of demonstration, by doing so they undermine the constitutional parameters in which the right to demonstrate operates. The moment when the participants departed the constitutional means, the legality of the activity can be highly questioned. Violent demonstrations weigh heavily against state development and prosperity. The rampage activities are not only bad, but cancerous activities which paralyze society and incapacitate the natives. It is important to note that, peaceful demonstrations and peace protests lead to a compromise as a stepping stone and a great vision for the future as a goal, whereas rampage and violent demonstrations lead to destruction and death in the process and bloodshed as a yield. It will be good and highly desirable for individuals to live in a state of perpetual peace through upholding the constitutional means of opposing the repressive and regressive agenda, wise use of residual power to control the government without display a presumptuous move of inviting violence. Foreboding and calamitous consequences of violent demonstrations are: due to the failure of citizens to keep their heads on top of bad economic waters of the nation, they resorted in invoking the radical means which destined them to the oasis of blood as a terrible response dispatched from the incumbent power holders, this amounts to unspeakable outcomes which sow the seeds of anger among citizens. Not only that, violent demonstrations divide society into different segments which reflects a polarized society. Apter (1997) stresses that, "among its most negative effects is the reinforcement of prejudiced boundaries. For political violence not only divides people, it polarizes them around affiliations..." Fundamentally, political violence in the form of violent demonstrations is a death blow to the workings and network of society. Violent demonstrations cannot only polarize society, it also creates a new form of society whereby people vie each other as political foes. In Apter's words, political violence leaves a 'retrievable anger' among people. Within a same polity, enormity and prosperity go in opposite directions. A society marked by groups of people who are divided and polarized around the zone of affiliation will never prosper but backwardness becomes the birth right of that society. In the nation, there is a functional relationship between politics and violent demonstrations, dangerous correlation which affects the position of the economy that already mired in recession. A cleansing agent is required which purify politics and absolutely separate the field from violent demonstrations that is a strong courage and determination to introduce smart politics. Cordiality, unity, and cooperation are relic of peace and genuine politics, while enormity, disunity, and lack of oneness cannot be read without violence. Social solidarity is a pre-emptive measure against violent demonstrations and without it the nation turned to be a country, a shelter of political foes roar behind each other aiming to occupy the zenith position. Nau (2012), in international relations connotation notes that, without solidarity, communities divide and development becomes oppression as many failed states experience. To put it in local context, without social solidarity, communities divide and development becomes oppression as many failed state experiences. Zimbabweans must stop violent demonstrations and rampage activities, casting a blind eye to parallel lines of affiliations, work for unity and restore genuine politics that is a way to new Zimbabwe. A covetous for stable politics, and pleasant political environment should be instantaneously develop as depicted in the other nations that are champions in liberal democracy.

MAGNIFICENT POPULAR RULE

The question about democratic nature of the nation is another cornerstone which anchor distorted politics and series of political instability therefore, ambivalent discussion is needed to pave way for new Zimbabwe. Schumpeters (1979), define democracy as an institutional arrangement in which those who occupy public offices should be granted permission from the masses through a competitive struggle for peoples' vote. The election platform, and the circumstances and conditions around it do not typify the manifestation of all democratic principles. The platform comes once in a five year period, and the masses cast ballot in support of the individuals among the alternatives but this is not enough. The degree of representation and the position of the masses towards governmental power are yardstick tenets of democracy which in most cases remain in illusion. More attention should be given to the degree of representation which have the following consequences: development begins at societal level, this pushes the government to focus on national issues as the local managed to stand firmly on the ground and champion initiatives, lack of representation or representation in a pipedream way paralyzes the ability of a society to function and jeopardize the potentialities of self-sufficient development. Politics used to be perquisite for the rich property owners, but as long as the election platform used to be the process for the recruitment of the bureaucratic class, the nation will suffer from serious economic hardships as the recruitment will stand as an obstacle to the self-sufficiency of the society. The intermediary parliamentarians: those who elected to represent the constituencies at local level, should always be in a position to spearhead development at the constituency level. This is a true symbol of representation. It is well known that the government is there to represent the interest of the nation, however, the national interest can only be attained if the government is a good listener to the grievances of the citizens. It is much relevant to highlight many tenets of democracy in this discussion, but the central point is not to discuss all well-known tenets rather the essay is targeting surreptitious angles of democracy which remain in illusion. The illusionary of some democratic principles create half-baked meal of democracy that turn to be a pivot for disputation among political institutions. The nations that follow democracy and adopt it as their political culture record high degree of success in all sectors including economy.

SUCCINCT SUMMARY

From this chapter it is crucial to note that, Zimbabwean politics is characterized by ceaseless election contestations which has an adverse impact in citizen participation in political activities and processes. Although the survey conducted by Schlee (2011) on protest participation denotes that the percentage of respondents who would attend demonstration or protest march increased by six percent from 2004 to 2006 leaves a room for prognosis of continuous increase in attendants in the preceded years, however, the participation of citizens in political activities nowadays remain urban centred juxtapose the rural people who stay level-headed with the pain of penetrating economic quagmire which worsen their suffering and social unrest. Political system defined by the rise of bureaucracy, political violence as evidenced by violent demonstration of 15 January 2019, ceaseless election contestations, and allegations of election skulduggery all together creates inconspicuous political environment which largely correlate with economic recession and meltdown. The question around the issue of democracy is another source of political upheavals. Tocqueville (1945) notes that democracy needs to be 'purified'. It is the duty of the incumbent regime and other political institutions to purify democracy so that the nation will stop to follow the odd. Zimbabweans should be assiduous to restore genuine politics and stable political grounds in order to rescue the economic vehicle which is completely mired in recession. Unless citizen participation is absolutely guaranteed or unless the regime in power adhere to the guiding principles of democracy, politics will remain a field of contestations, and worsen discontent among citizens due to its adverse effects on economy and peoples' livelihood therefore, society will remain deeply divided and heavily transfixed. The chapters subsequent to this discussion are ratiocination pieces of writing which incisively assess the correlation between politics and economy.

CORRELATION 0F POLITICS AND ECONOMY

'Citizens evaluate politicians' performance by using macroeconomic indicators as yardsticks' Mugge (2016).

Zimbabwe's economy began to fall soon after the attainment of independence in 1980. A number of economic policies and reforms were implemented but in vain. The economy continued to decline but with little bit ups and downs. The average of ups and downs depict the gradual fall of economy up until it sat in the dish of recession in the year 2000 and onwards (reflection from the superficial analysis of the nation's statistics of Gross Domestic Product (GDP) from the ministry of economic and other various sources). The actions which the incumbent regime and its leaders took by then pictured the neo Marxism approach: an approach which focuses on the economic reforms and policies to address the economic structure. This can be evidenced by the number of economic reforms and policies which were implemented time and again in order to correct the teetering economy. The failure of the neo Marxism approach to redeem the Zimbabwean economy from incessant recession speaks a lot to the citizens and leaders. Since the approach has been tested and verified for a long period of time, but reflecting its weaknesses to bring economic changes, there is need to cognizant other approaches. The point here is that, Zimbabwean economy cannot correct itself through reforms which are largely imparted to its structure alone, then there is need to invite the external one that is political perspective. It is important to note that, during try and error era when economic reforms stalled the signals of political reforms, the political field were ultimately distorted. The economic challenges were not linked to economic structure, and even in the present moment, therefore, the implementation of economic reforms is necessary but in the Zimbabwean context can be summed up as a prescription for the wrong illness. The economic turbulence which affect the nation is a result of distorted politics. Unless the economic reforms and policies for the present moment become an erstwhile subject, while the prerequisite of political reforms lead from the front, the nation will remain mired in recession. Politics is a yardstick determinant factor for the transformation of economy. Challenges that hampering the nation from recording a tremendous economic revival and transformation are linked to politics. The imbroglio political environment defined by widespread social ramification, and ceaseless election contestations completely outweigh the capacity of the nation to develop economically. It is therefore cogent that, the economic recession witnessed in the nation for a long period of time is a result of wrongs in politics. In other words, there is a cause and effect relationship between politics and economy. The cause and effect relationship is not just a hypothetical assumption but an alternative hypothesis which can be tested, verified, and falsified in the Zimbabwean context. The political stability together with conducive political grounds is a prerequisite condition to be achieved and maintained before the implementation of economic reforms and policies. There is the possibility that the significance of the magnificent economic reforms or policies can be turned down by the prevailing political conditions of the day. The struggle for Zimbabweans should be a struggle for correction of wrongs in politics: political antagonism, ceaseless election contestations, grapevine, which deteriorates political institutions. Politics in Zimbabwean context stand as a smoke scream that hide economic recession. It is difficult, if not impossible to have economic revival and transformation if the wrongs in politics goes unchallenged. For the present moment, people are pointing fingers to the variety of bewildering issues blaming them for the economic meltdown, for instance corruption, inconsistence of economic reforms and policies, and the failure of the incumbent regime in general but all these are products of unstable politics.

ILLUSTRATION FOR STATISTICAL VINDICATION

Without delving in the discussion of politics of the nation as it was already expressed in the previous chapter, it is important at this juncture to show the close correlation of politics and economy. The correlation shed light on the reasons for the failure of economic reforms and policies to uplift the economy from the underneath recession zone. The economic reforms and policies are more of a pain therapy which ease the pain without curing the disease, recession and meltdown are largely embedded on a political rock. The crux of this paper is to show the relationship between politics and economy that is stable politics result in stable economy and unstable politics cause unstable economy. Table 1.2 is a list of Gross Domestic Product (GDP) growth rate from 2007 up to 2013.

Table 1.2: GDP growth rate from 2007 to 2013.

Years	GDP growth rate
2007	-3,3
2008	-14
2009	5,4
2010	11,4
2011	11,9
2012	10,6
2013	4,5

Source: *African Development Bank Database and the Ministry of Finance.*

The tabulated data show economic position of the nation basing on fundamental data release indicator GDP growth rate in each specific year. The graphical illustration in fig 1.2 intends to unravel the tabulated data which reflects the economic position of the nation from 2007 to 2013.

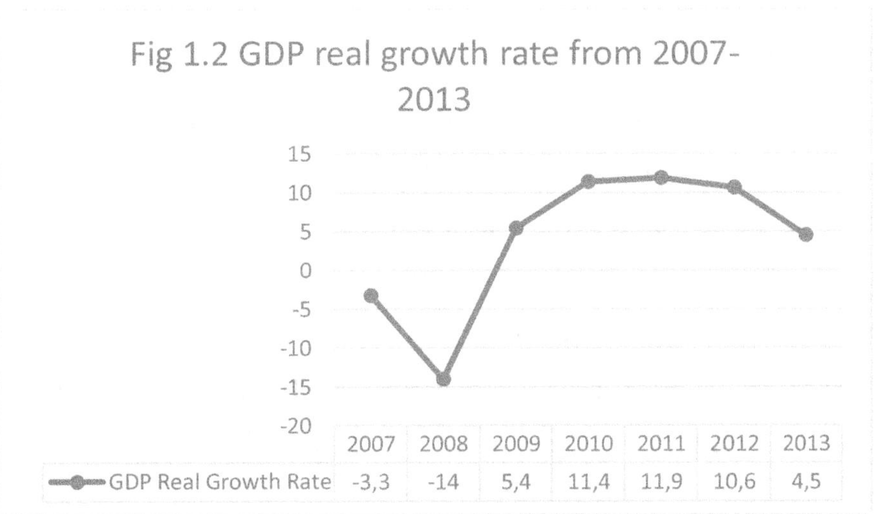

Source: *Africa Development Bank Database and the Ministry of Finance.*

As illustrated in fig 1.2 above, the economic growth of the nation as measured by the main macroeconomic indicator GDP growth rate defined by extreme negative fall and exponential rise from 2007 to 2013. In this analysis of correlation of politics and economy, the 2007 to 2013 timeframe suffices to be used as a starting point of the discussion so as to lay the mate of paradoxical relationship between politics and economy. In the graph, 2007 to 2013 period enshroud two election years that were characterized by distinct political environment and distinguished outcomes. The 2008 elections were marked by changeable electoral history and the 2013 witnessed the huffy news of the rejection of election outcomes. From the graph, it is crucial to highlight that there is a precipitous fall of GDP growth rate in 2007 and 2008 with an astonishing negative record of -14. The surprising fall in GDP growth rate can be attributed to the political environment and the general order of the politics of the day. In 2008, the nation experienced a petulant change in political environment. Masunungure (2009) describes 27 June 2008 elections as 'militarized elections'. This evinced obnoxious, ferocious and inconspicuous political environment that waxed the horrendous fall in GDP leading to low economic progress record. The negative GDP growth rate in 2008 largely correlate to the then prevailing political environment

INDELIBLE ERA

From 2009 to 2013 stable or genuine politics invigorated economy of the nation and the lustrous GDP growth rate is the tangible evidence. This line of argument is pertinent when one compare 2008 political conditions together with the economic results to that of 2009 to 2011. Of a great surprise, in 2009 the nation recorded a shocking rise of GDP growth rate with 5.4 percent. The table 1.3, below shows GDP growth rate of 2009 to 2013.

Table 1.3: GDP real growth rate from 2009 to 2013.

Yeas	GDP growth rate
2009	5,4
2010	11,4
2011	11,9
2012	10,6
2013	4,5

Source: *Africa Development Bank Database and the Ministry of Finance.*

Table 1.3 shows the staggering GDP growth rate from 2009 up to 2011 and a shocking fall towards an election year. The tabulated data above is presented in the graph below.

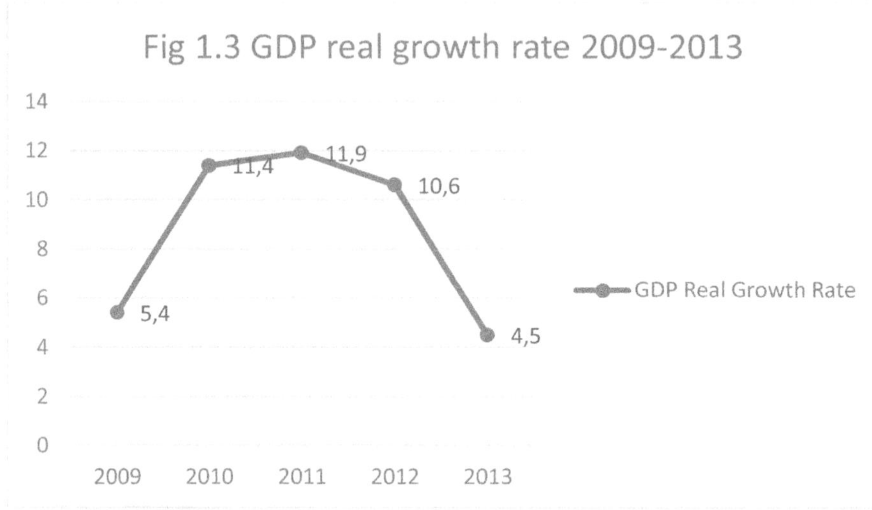

As illustrated in fig 1.3, from 2009 to 2013, Zimbabwe recorded positive GDP growth rate. The reason behind this tremendous record was instantaneous change in politics and political environment, a great transformation from imbroglio political environment to harmony, unity, and cooperation among political institutions. This was because of the global political agreement which resulted in the formation of the Government of National Unity. The United Nations report (2011), stresses that the economic growth in Zimbabwe from 2009 attributed to the political reforms reflected by the formation of the Government of National Unity. The government of national unity and the transitional authority stupendously transformed societal organization, this resulted in the reduction in widespread of social ramification nonetheless conducive environment which was prone for economic activities was created. The 2009 to 2013 era can be credited as illustrious era whereby stable politics as defined by peace, unity, cooperation, and harmony illuminated the economic field. It is important to note that, stable politics stimulate a feeling of consensus nation building among citizens which brings in revival and transformation in the economic position of the nation. The year 2011 as shown in the graph with 11,9 percent GDP growth rate can be credited as the magnificent year in which the nation recorded buoyant economic level. Why there was an instant fall in GDP growth rate from 2012 to 2013? The answer to this question is that, from 2011 political institutions were endowed with the spirit of power hence, they started to part ways from each other, vibrant shock to cooperation which then undermine development as progression turned to be regression leading to unanticipated economic slowdown. The post 2013 political environment failed to rescue the economic ship from being mired in recession because the election outcomes conform to the profound custom of disputed results. The outcomes again cast the nation into the old route of poor economic performance. A debate is likely to arise on the notion that the horrendous rise of GDP growth rate from -14 in 2008 to 11,9 in 2011 was whether eventuated by economic reforms particularly the introduction of multi-currency system or an end product of political order. A point to note is that the introduction of multi-currency system in 2009 counter-point to stable politics, was yardstick economic drive. The grim news of economic reforms did nothing except to register for the accomplish fate. As indicated by the surprising rise in GDP growth rate from 2009 to 2011, no extra effort can be required to cogent Zimbabweans that, politics determine economy, therefore, the political field is a prerequisite side to be addressed first before the implementation of economic reforms.

FEASIBLE FORMULA

Conspicuous political ground + economic reforms = buoyant economy.

The introduction of economic reforms without conspicuous political ground, the idea is foredoomed from start. In other words, in Zimbabwean context, economic reforms cannot be equal to buoyant economy but rather buoyant economy is the end product of the perfect assimilation of economic reforms into the lucrative grounds of politics. This point is pertinent as the 2009 to 2013 era stands as a proven formula. It is not good enough for the nation to focus on the introduction of economic reforms and policies on the distorted grounds of politics. Those who purport that, the implementation of strong economic reforms and policies together with the deathblow to policy inconsistence is key for economic revival and transformation are right, what matters most is not valid and worthiness of reforms or policies but the ground on which they are applied. As already proved in the past, and indicated in the graph, in the years of peace, unity, cooperation, and stability the nation recorded a significant rise in GDP growth rate. What can be done to rescue the nation from recession? The answer to this question is stable politics. Stable politics result in stable economy and unstable politics is the real mentor of economic quagmire.

EBB AND FLOW RUN

To strengthen the correlation of politics and economy, there is need to show the Zimbabwean run from 2004 up to 2014. The table 1.4 below shows the list of GDP growth rate in respect to a specific year.

Table 1.4: GDP real growth rate from 2004 to 2014.

Years	GDP Growth Rate
2004	3,8
2005	-4,1
2006	-3,6
2007	-3,3
2008	-14
2009	5,4
2010	11,4
2011	11,9
2012	10,6
2013	4,5
2014	3,8

Source: *United Nations Commission for Africa, Ministry of Finance, and African Development Bank Database.*

Fig 1.4 is a graphical data presentation of the information presented in table 1.4 above.

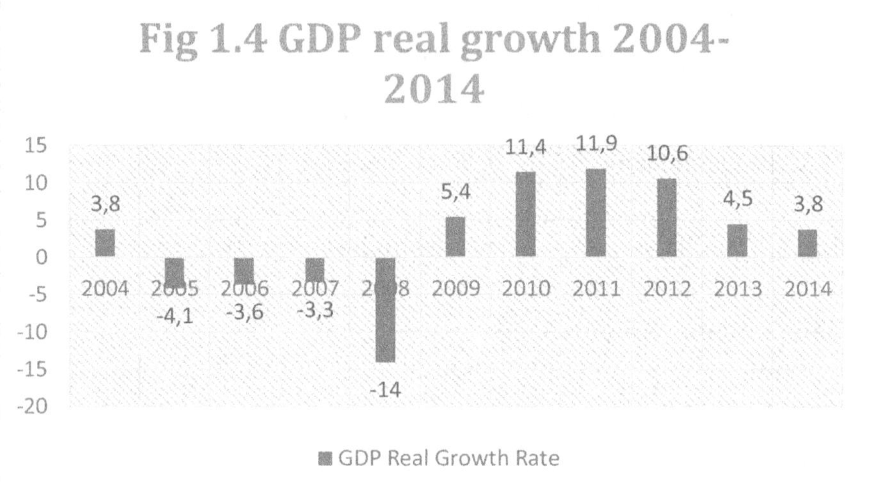

Source: *United Nations Commission for Africa, Ministry of Finance, and African Development Bank Database.*

The fig 1.4 above is an illustration of Zimbabwe GDP growth rate run from 2004 up to 2014. In general the run marked by ups and downs which in average depict poor economic performance. From 2004 to 2007, the nation recorded a negative growth of GDP, and in 2008 the nation was completely mired in recession with a horrendous -14 GDP growth rate. This depicts the dangers of unstable politics to economic growth. The inconspicuous political environment, particularly the records of first and second phases of elections that is 29 March and 27 June 2008 respectively had an adverse impact on economy. Politics and economy cannot be read in isolation and their correlation extend to the fact that, when politics is unstable the economic structure will follow the tune, and the opposite is true. At this point, beyond doubt, one can conclude that the economic challenges that hampering the nation from following the path of progress and targeting Sustainable Development Goals is linked to politics. To shed more light on the relationship between politics and economy, the period from 2009 to 2011 can stand as tangible evidence. That is to say because of stable politics as a result of coalition between political giants the nation recorded a shocking rise in GDP growth rate. All economic challenges that heavily affected the nation in 2008 viz: indexation, inflation, unemployment, to mention a few, were engulfed by stable political conditions of 2009 hence, sudden rise and a positive record of GDP growth rate. By tracing a trend of GDP growth rate from 2004 up to 2014, one can note that the trend fall towards every election year, this reinforces the point that the economic position of the nation largely correlate with the politics of the day. A panacea to the Zimbabwean crises is a gutsy for the restoration of genuine politics. From the analysis of an economic run from 2004 to 2014, the graph is characterized by precipitous fall and horrendous rise in GDP growth rate. It is important to note that, the proliferation of socio-economic challenges went hand in hand with the enormous rise of political turbulence towards an election year and post period in some instances. A good example is the period prior and aftermath 2013 elections. With reference to fig 1.4, it is proven that the GDP growth rate rise in the conducive political grounds for instance, 2009 to 2011 era due to the influence of coalition of major political institutions. The coalition played a critical role of settling down the dust of political turmoil which was created by the whirlwind of imbroglio political environment of 2008. There is no need of special glasses to see the fundamental role of stable politics in spearheading development. Stable politics is the way of attaining economic revival and transformation particularly in the context of Zimbabwe, although people cognizant economic reforms and policies as chief factors behind a staggering economic growth of 2009 to 2011. It is not erroneous to describe the introduction of economic reforms and policies to end economic meltdown as a pre-conceived idea which is no longer fit in the current state of politics. The ideas of economist, particularly in the past temporal, set a precedent of economic reforms and policies as key determinants behind socio-economic development. Nowadays the precedence failed to accomplish the prevailing wave of politics as key determinant factor, rather economic reforms work counter-point to the political situation. The pre-dominant of economic reforms and policies can be put into consideration without ignoring the prevailing political environment. The likelihood of economic reforms and policies to cause change in socio-economic sphere is very low, but their co-existence with good political environment significantly transform the nation, with politics as an outstanding prerequisite. Bratton and Rothchild (1992:263) underscore that, "the social scientists dealing with Africa development have used to concentrate on economic issues while overlooking the highly important political dimension process." The true answer to the ceaseless economic turbulence is stable politics. The political institutions should address the issue of distorted politics first before any attempt to rebuild economic structure through the implementation of reforms and policies which are greatly imparted to the structure of economy.

TOWARDS THE NEW DISPENSETION

The political environment and Gross Domestic Product growth rate from 2014 up to 2018 evinced the correlation between politics and economy, as politics remain outstanding field which requires attention and reforms in order to drive the economic vehicle from recession to buoyant state. The table 1.5 shows GDP growth rate from 2014 up to 2018.

Table 1.5: GDP real growth rate from 2014 to 2018.

Years	GDP Growth Rate
2014	3,8
2015	1,5
2016	0,8
2017	4,7
2018	6,2

Source: Zimstat

The table 1.5, shows the GDP growth rate from 2014 to 2018. The tabulated data is presented in the graph below.

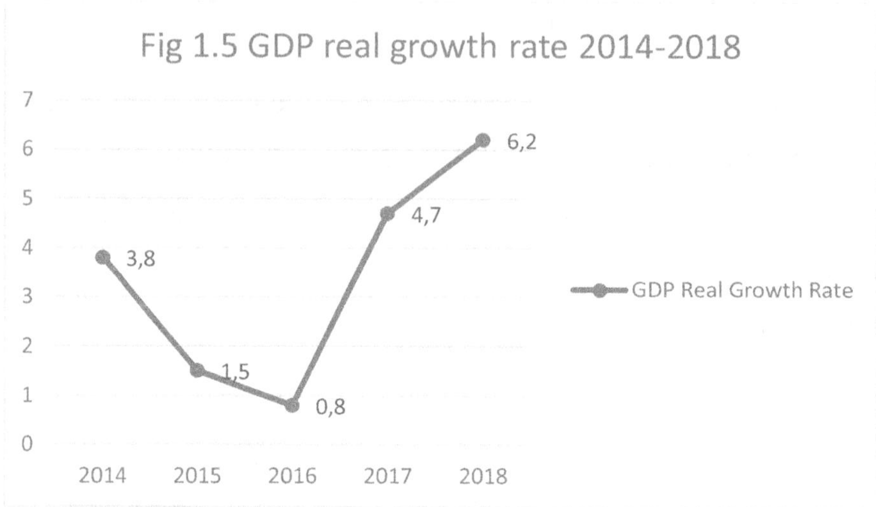

Fig 1.5 GDP real growth rate 2014-2018

Source: Zimstat

A close examination to fig 1.5 denotes that GDP growth rate fall from 3.8 in 2014 to 0.8 in 2016. Subsequently, there is an exponential growth from 4.7 in 2017 to 6.2 in 2018. At this juncture it is imperative to show correlation of politics and economy. In spite of strong economic reforms and policies that were implemented in the years 2014, 2015, and 2016, the GDP growth rate recorded a shocking fall up to 0.8 in 2016. From a political perspective, the shocking fall in GDP growth rate from 2014 to 2016 largely linked to distorted politics and bad political environment. This was because of 2013 elections which produce a disputed outcome as per Zimbabwe Election Support Network report hence, the nation compensate the impasse with poor economic performance as a charge intended to cover the state of politics. The bad political environment as a result of disputed election outcomes incapacitate the citizens resulting in enormous fall of GDP growth rate hence, slowdown of economy. The year 2016 with 0.8 GDP growth rate, stands as a turning point in the five year run and the nation started to record a staggering rise aftermath. The reason behind a superlative growth recorded in 2017 is a political one although efforts made to revive the economy through introduction of measures and policies which were largely linked to its structure play significant role. The year 2016 was a turning point for both politics and economy. The turning point in politics that is transformation of political environment was a paramount factor behind astounding rise in GDP growth rate from 0.8 percent to 4.7 percent in 2017. In 2016, the memories of the disputed 2013 election results undergone a gradual dissipation and all political institutions stampeded into campaign for the preparation of 2018 elections. A stable political environment in disguise which was conducive for the economic growth was temporarily established. This caused a remarkable rise of GDP growth rate up to 2018. Although, at the end of 2018 inflation and price hikes, commemorative agents of 2008 dogged the nation, the Operation Restore Legacy exhilaration remain a substantial feature which then give rise to GDP growth rate up to 6.2 percent. The trend of GDP growth rate from 2014 up to 2018 denotes that politics is a prerequisite move to address the economic challenges that hampering the nation from targeting Millennium Development Goals as well as achieving sustainable ones. The fact that, endemic problems that dogged the nation have meaning, there is need to employ logical positivism approach to accomplish the challenges. There is need to assess the problems then deduce meaning and finally use logical thinking to end the challenges. From fig 1.5, it is shown that, GDP growth rate fall when the nation was characterized by odious political environment. An assessment of a closer link between political environment and economy exposes the meaning of the problems. It is vital to conclude then that, inflation, indexation, volatile exchange rates, and unchecked corruption are outcomes of distorted politics which affect the beam of economy. Subsequent to the finding of the meaning of the problems then the application of logical thinking to end the problems. In this case, the root cause is politics, then the logical thinking implies that, to address politics as a broader rock on which economic challenges are embedded there is need to cure the root cause of unstable politics through knowledge and understanding to cut unexpected widespread of social complexities, restoration of trust, justice, fairness, and accountability to end election contestations. Finally, a finding path to new Zimbabwe which can cause great complacency among the citizens.

UNITY A PHENOMENAL MODUS VIVENDI

This part intends to emphasize the importance of unity, and cooperation among political institutions and its impact on economy. Rapport and rapprochement among political institutions are key issues that are very important for the revival and transformation of economy. Before one venture into details about the importance of unity and cooperation among political institutions whereas the former is exceptionally yardstick, a starting point is to illustrate three graphs showing GDP growth rate of three distinct five year periods. The table below present data of GDP growth rate in respect to a particular five year period.

Table 1.6: GDP real growth rate of distinct five year periods 2004-2008, 2009-2013 and 2014-2018.

2004-2008 GDP	2009-2013 GDP	2014-2018 GDP
3,8	5,4	3,8
-4,1	11,4	1,5
-3,6	11,9	0,8
-3,3	10,6	4,7
-14	4,5	6,2

Source: *United Nations Economic Commission for Africa Report, Africa Development Bank Database, and Zimstat.*

The data from table 1.6 is presented in the three graphs below. Each graph shows the specific five year period. In essence the graphs intend to demonstrate the importance of cooperation and unity among political institutions. This paper is in support of the view that economic challenges that affect the nation for a long period of time are perpetrated by distorted politics, therefore to address political side amounts to a clear restoration of socio-economic order. This line of argument is pertinent when one cognizant the data presented in table 1.6, and then deduce a clear and palpable assessment. The graphs A, B, and C below represent different timeframes that is 2004-2008, 2009-2013, and 2014-2018 respectively.

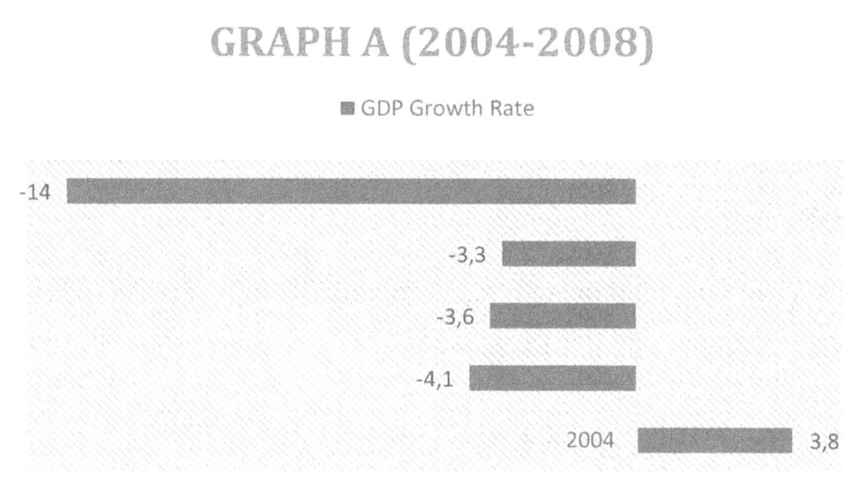

The graph A illustrates the trend of GDP growth rate from 2004 to 2008, the point here is not to take figures as it is but the main concern is about what the trend tells citizens about the link between GDP growth rate and the political wave of the time.

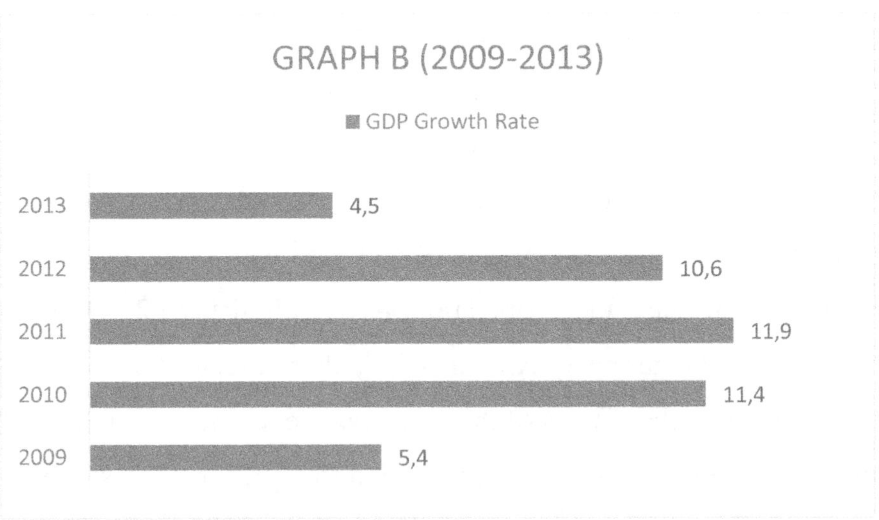

The graph B, shows the results of the 2009 to 2013 era of economic position of the nation.

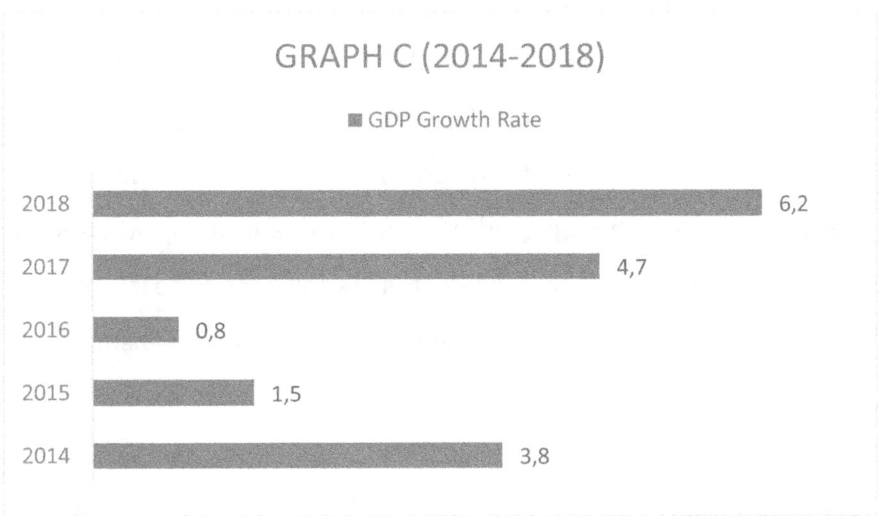

A close examination of three graphs A, B, and C shows that all are distinct to each other marked by different GDP growth rate. Among the three, the graph A has a least GDP growth, followed by C and B is a superlative record of the nation with unprecedented GDP growth rate since the year 2000. Before delving into the implications of the three distinctive graphs, it is important at this juncture to show the reasons for the variation and deviation of GDP growth rate as illustrated in the three graphs A, B, and C as well as to cement the significant of unity and cooperation. Above all, the era 2009-2013, recorded a staggering growth in GDP, therefore it stands as the better epoch in the history of the nation, however, better is not good enough there is still unmitigated demand to fight for the best which is yet to come as this paper tries to open a new path anchored on stable political choreographic pattern. Subsequently, the 2014-2018 era is second from a distinguished era which automatically second to none, whereas the 2004-2008 era is the worse, an odious era characterized by negative growth. The categorization of the above mentioned timeframes into different eras helps to present tangible argument, although the term era in most cases refer to an indeterminate length of period of time, in this case is indicating a five year timeframe. The fundamental point here is to evince the importance of unity and cooperation among political institutions. The generality of a paradoxical link between distorted politics and low economic performance has been already exhausted in the previous discussions. The central point at this juncture is, in totality, to make a comparison of the three graphs A, B, and C with the intention to strengthen the importance of unity and cooperation among political institutions. A special attention should be directed to the focal life of Zimbabweans in the distinct eras because the years of life in the obnoxious political environment does not matter but the life of years in the shadow of an unbearable circumstances matters most, with the intention to seek a lasting solution and to compensate the harsh moments with magnificent lifestyle, hence, there is need to look beyond a displayed political picture frame. In 2009, the pre-dominant old-system of the winner takes all which defines power relations among political institutions were superseded by a rapprochement pact: an agreement between major political institutions which resulted in the formation of the Government of National Unity (GNU). The fact that, the pact was short lived, makes the period 2009-2013 to be described as a revolving door in which the political institutions instantaneously fall into a special form of organization which last for a short period of time. There is need to point out the fruits of the GNU that Zimbabweans reap namely: level of economic success although it cannot be overemphasized, and conspicuous political environment that characterized a revolving door period. A great emphasis should be given to the exceptional move of political institutions to form a coalition which portrays genuine politics. The relative political stability ameliorated the economic trend which was in a tailspin. In other words, the rise in GDP growth rate from 2009-2013 was facilitated by the formation of the Government of National Unity that evinces conducive environment for economic growth. The superlative rise of GDP growth rate in 2009, which continued to accelerate up to 2011 coincide with the political order of the day particularly unity among other features. Amicable relationship between political institutions amid amiable environment was yardstick for the horrendous rise in GDP growth rate. This depicts that unity among political institutions is the exact way to revive and transform economy as evidenced by the GDP growth rate in graph B which is completely distinguished from other graphs, therefore, graph B is illustrious one that cement the importance of unity and cooperation for economic transformation. Therefore, tractable economic challenges are very simple to deal with, taking advantage of suffice and ample resources, the agreeable political environment is needed to champion the route of development and entrench all economic hindrance. At this far, it is crucial to note that economic turbulence is closely linked to politics. Fixing politics is to kill two birds with one stone that is to address causes and consequences at the same time. Graphs A and C depict the impact of lack of oneness, unity and cooperation among political institutions. The five year period of diverging opinions and animosity among political institutions can be summed up as a dry era which produces nothing novel or interesting that is the indication of other graphs particularly A. The irony is that the end of amicable relationship among political institutions went hand in hand with the fall of GDP growth rate. The intricacy of economic pattern from 2004 up to 2018 is a matter of vigorous changes in the political stance. This stands as another tangible evidence which support the view that politics and economy are paradoxically compatible to each other. It is crucial to note that, the collapse of the rapprochement pact categorizes the political institutions and ignited a war-race of superiority complex and restarts proliferation of economic challenges as evidenced by a shocking fall of GDP growth rate to approximately 4,5 percent in 2013. Unless the intestinal fortitude among political institutions suffice, the economic turbulence which coincide with politics will remain as a stumbling block for the nation to record significant and substantial development that can be credited with meteoric.

This chapter assesses the correlation between politics and economy that is the cause and effect relationship between the two. In other words, one can point such a correlation as a paradoxical relationship from which a disputation and tendentious argument is likely to arise posit to the different cause of economic crisis in the nation. This paper as it tackling Zimbabwe economic crisis from a political perspective other perception cannot be refuted, however, the degree of validity and credibility of such perception in relation to causality can be highly cognizant. All the data presented in this chapter suffice to show that the economic turbulence that affect the nation is linked to politics. The solution is to deal with the politics in order to establish conducive political environment. As it stands now, opening a business in Zimbabwe is a stressful thing, not because of management and highly demanding commitment but because of volatile exchange rates and incalculable inflation rate. In sum, it is not good enough to end the discussion of the correlation suggesting that the way to abandon the economic mess is to address political side without providing the exact way of dealing with distorted politics. Acemoglu and Robinson (2012) note that, improved health and life expectancy were not the cause of England's economic success but one of the fruits of its previous political and economic changes. The subsequent chapters provide the exact way of creating conspicuous political environment.

INQUISITIVE FOR A NEW ROUTINE

The electoral process and election activities had a history of sowing a seed of ceaseless election contestations. The process and activities channelized unstable politics, hold the contentment of the citizens in suspension, while stultification, discontent and resentment registering to the ever ending triteness. With such unbearable circumstances thanks should be given to the Zimbabweans who avoided cataclysm under the shadow of populism at all cost. The avoidance of cataclysm does not mean that citizens do not have dream for change. Change remains an ambitious thing and a particular way to transform marginalized social circles. In this paper, regular conduct of elections is presented as another angle that produce distorted politics. The problem is to find a lasting solution to divert political vehicle from following the old choreography and directed it to the new routine. Because of ceaseless election contestation records, buoyant economy was made the taboo subject for a long period of time, subsequent to that, economic turbulence taint the economic position of the nation. What can be done to restore socio-economic order? Remains a question which needs to be treated with a minute of accuracy. The parallel lines that demarcate the operation of political institutions make the question to be tendentious. It is not fallacious to sum up politics and political activities as a hocus-pocus game because of the complicated things that are indecipherable. Divisions and hostility are intrinsically inseparable with political institutions that always vie each other as a political foe. A sublime and working solution is required to deciphering politics and political activities and to set a novel trajectory.

AN ELECTION CYCLE

It is a state practice to conduct regular elections akin to the democratic customs and practices. The core issue is to end abhorrent practice that imperil political institutions. At this moment, it is imperative to propose a panacea which can solve the issue of election contestations and lay the foundation for Zimbabwe we want. It is crucial to highlight that elections together with the situation that surrounds the electoral process notably pre and post environment is an interconnected events. Such interconnectivity can be arranged to produce interrelated parts which make a cycle. The diagram below corroborates.

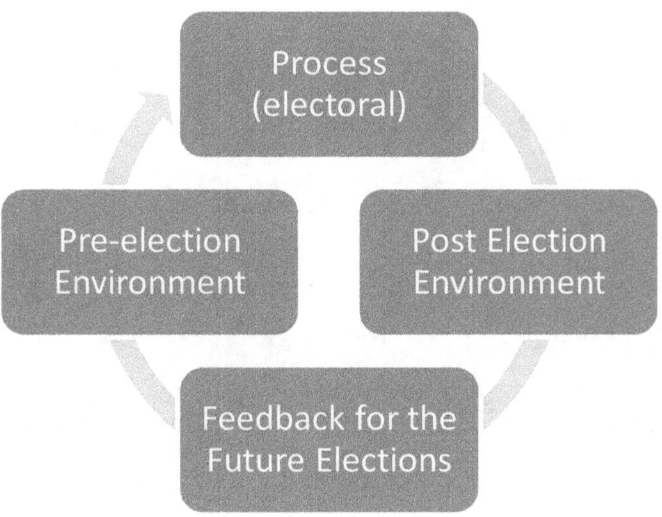

The diagram above, pictures an isolated parts which are closely linked to each other. The diagram intends to show the basis for the development of distorted politics. The fact that, the parts are connected to each other in terms of their function and influence, they depict a complete static cycle that permeate the political environment of the nation. The pre-election environment determines the way in which process can be done. Similarly, the way in which elections are conducted shapes the post political environment, and the future results are inclined to both pre and post environment.

Why elections in Zimbabwe are failing to deliver?

Elections in Zimbabwe are failing to deliver in a number of ways:

-Rejection of election outcomes that show an electoral process impasse (an election stalemate drama).

-Endless squabble among political gladiators over election outcomes that typify an empty bickering.

-Exacerbated incessant economic recession soon after elections.

-Polarization and entrenched societal division along political affiliation prejudices.

The question about the failure of elections to deliver is very tendentious and subject to disputation. The solution to curtail the issue of election contestations is to deal with the pre-election environment to ensure conduciveness of the environment. The conspicuous political environment can be created when political institutions reach a compromise guided by amicable conditions amid agreeable environment in general. The failure to create suitable political conditions from the onset amounts for a recipe of imbroglio political conditions. The solutions to address the issue of election contestation are incisively discussed in the next sub-chapter.

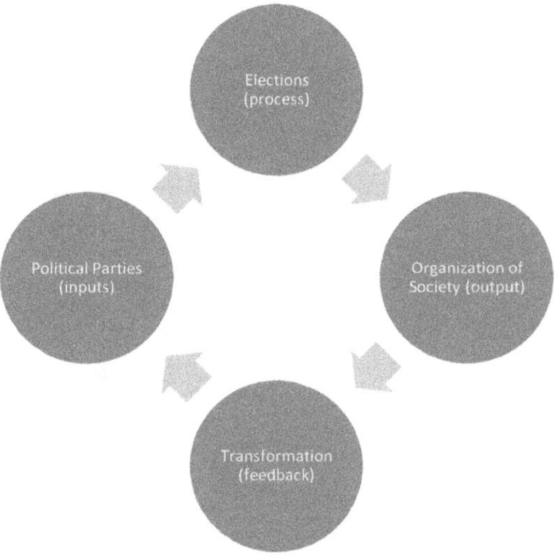

Meanwhile, the diagram above is a cycle that shows Zimbabwe political matrix and the bottom line is to work out pragmatic approach that ensures the workability of the cycle in changing the lives of the people. The cycle denotes how politics correlate with economy. The organization of society is key for transformation in the social and economic sectors. Political institutions together with the playing field (electoral process) are determinants of the future position of the communities. The transformation part in the cycle is the mirror to review the degree of progress particularly by looking at the fundamentals of economy. Unless the root cause of unstable politics is detected and addressed, the contemporaneous of economic turbulence and the tenacity of ossified distorted political system is unavoidable. The stick-to-itiveness of the concomitant will make the locus of politics cause celebre.

REFORMS: APPRAISAL AND EMPHASIS

The sources of political problems that then generate economic crisis are elections and electoral process. The custom and practice of having regular elections are now become the tailwind behind political vehicle. The only way to make the dust of political turbulence completely settle is to understand how political cycle works. It is not fallacious to note that allegation of voter intimidation, election skulduggery, massaging of votes, lack of accountability and transparency and the plaintive call for free and fair elections characterize Zimbabwean electoral process. All these are exigible political traits that demand electoral process to follow a new choreographic pattern distanced from changeable electoral history record. Good performance comes after reforms, real electoral reforms is the path to transform the past. Rumbling and crying for electoral and political reforms are entirely social conscience, fundamental areas that generate skirmishes among political institutions. As it stands now, the five year regular interval period of elections is a political cycle which produce nothing except the seeds of antagonism and unresolved political dispute. The problem is to find a lasting solution to address the challenges that hinder the political cycle from delivering to the society. The elimination of profound challenge, real seed that causes political dispute is a fundamental work required. Society and political institutions will continue to suffer from the pain of disunity and ceaseless disagreements if the real problem that brood distorted politics goes unchallenged. The pre-emptive way to challenge the central causes of disputed elections and unstable politics is the introduction of political reforms. Political reforms can help the nation to abandon the old fashioned track and stigmatized way of handling elections which is the heart of disputed politics. The superficial analysis of election records from time to time reflect that elections and electoral process are the chief causes of distorted politics. The direct way of eliminating the distorted part is to address the electoral process through the introduction of strong and effective reforms. Reforms which transform the electoral process from inconsistent record to the genuine and transparency operation which solidify credibility of electorate's participation. As already indicated in the diagram of political cycle, the reason for the failure of elections to deliver to the people is the conditions and circumstances that surround the electoral system, therefore the introduction of reforms to correct such inconspicuous electoral environment facilitates the transformation that is the change in societal organization that then lure the economy to follow the tune. The degree of economic success therefore will depend upon the strength and weakness of the reforms. The socio-economic status in future without political reforms particularly that of electoral system are fore-doomed. No one can castigate the importance of reforms for societal transformation. Without imminent political reforms, the political vehicle will continue to follow the guaranteed traditional path, downthrown the citizens of the nation and worsen their benighted lifestyle. Political reforms, in spite of being epoch-making, they are essential in creating equable temperament among the masses, a step towards solid society. The introduction of political reforms is a gateway from economic recession as highlighted in the previous chapter of the correlation of politics and economy which corroborates the verdict that economic challenges are end products of distorted politics. It is only political reforms that can satisfy the longing thirst of better environment which necessitate the escalation of economic activities that then race hand in hand with maximum pleasure and luxurious life through flux economic growth. The long-standing and long-running economic hardships which cause long-suffering can be curtailed through the introduction of political reforms. It is a desire of each citizen to see New Zimbabwe. New Zimbabwe defined by buoyant economy, strong social fabric, and flourish of economic activities that is a sublime imaginable society that exist in air for long period of time. Political reforms for the present moment are the best alternative to bring it into manifestation. Unchecked political turbulence is now witnessed in the whole nation from the grassroots of society up to the bureaucracy, only reforms can make the alarming political turmoil saga collapsible, rolling and pill it to fit into the political reforming space. Due to the fact that, the political institutions are behind hand in introducing strong political reforms, the economic reforms and approaches are always belittled by the prevailing political environment. It is the political field which impetus bellicose among political institutions, a dangerous, aggressive, and warlike mood which affect the way in which people live. Political reforms is a death blow to bellicosity, a positive step towards unity, rapport, and oneness. With regard to the present state of social and economic status, political reforms preferably stand as alternative solution to restore social and economic order. The reason behind poor economic performance in the nation is distorted politics which need to be addressed through the introduction of political reforms.

TRANSFORMATION IN THE SOCIAL CIRCLES

The model of interconnected parts of political parties, process in the form of elections, societal organization and transformation are ordered in a way which symbolize political cycle. Parts are correctly arranged but the reason for the failure of politics to deliver to the people is a matter of conditions and circumstances behind the election competitions. Although, there are many possible permutation of politics, economy, and societal organization, the ordering way which brings transformation is: politics influencing societal organization, and the way in which society functions determine the degree of economic success.

The above process shows the permutation of three variables that correlate to each other. The political reforms are crucial to redefine the politics of the nation and politics determine the way in which society organized, the organization of society is yardstick for the degree of economic success. Unstable politics cause divided and polarized society, polarization incapacitate the citizens leading to economic slowdown hence, low degree of economic success. In contrast, stable politics create harmonious society characterized by agreeable political environment which is so conducive for economic activities necessary to boast productivity. As a result citizens can reap the fruits of buoyant economy. Although economic reforms that were implemented time and again are life-buoy for Zimbabweans, political field remains an outstanding field that calls for reforms. Unless elections conducted in a double-blind manner in which neither the commission nor the second person involved know not about the results, or unless the situation that surrounds the electoral process stop to be double-bind, elections will remain subject to ceaseless contestations and disputed politics.

THE BALANCING ACT CONCEPT

CONCEPTUAL CLARIFICATION

To outline the attributes of genuine and stable politics is not enough, the pragmatic approach to create stable politics in the nation is required. In a compartmentalized society with social complexities, and prejudice boundaries along lines of political affiliation, balancing act principle can be preferably stands as feasible solution. Zimbabwe can be regarded as a nation without social solidarity because of penetrating hot iron of division along the line of opinion and political affiliation. Such an ironic social conditions have doubled and reach the extremis level through the impact of the visible gap between the rich and poor. The gap between the rich and poor completes the definition of a compartmentalized society. The ordinary people suffers from the unacceptable negative activities of the few rich individuals who inherit the heir of oppression of men by men in the modernized society. As a result the position of the poor people continued to retard and worsen their inferiority complex. This is another angle which filter in social complexities the dangerous social position which heavily weigh against the economic position of the nation. The balancing act principle is the answer to such complications. It is the way to pull economic vehicle from recession towards a refulgent light of development.

INDIVIDUAL AND ECONOMIC MATRIX

The hardships and privation change citizens' natural disposition as they work to fit in the prevailing social and economic wave. The irritating part is that, due to the fact that most of Zimbabweans do not have food on the table, they resort in unlawful means to earn a living in the process they legalize the illegalities like corruption. The analogy of a food chain can incisively explain the situation in Zimbabwe. The fair distribution of energy in the food chain only happens if the source is sufficient to sustain the whole chain. In the context of Zimbabwe, although the source for the livelihood of all citizens suffice however, the total income per person is subjected to the variety of bewildering issues that include indexation, inflation, unjustified gyp, and volatile exchange rates. Indexation and inflation cause the income per person to be insufficient, for one to bounce back, he or she devices a mechanism that ends up legalize the illegalities in order to earn a living. The unchecked corruption reached the acme zoom for the present moment owing to inadequate income to sustain the worker and families therefore corruption is a last resort. Adam and Dyson (2003) note that, crime will be regarded not as wrong doing to be punished, but as an illness to be treated by help and understanding. Yes corruption is a crime, but it is an illness caused by economic turbulence that strike the nation therefore, it needs to be treated with help and understanding. The ceaseless engagement of citizens in illegal activities seems as if it is difficult to be stopped. The existing economic situation or environment is a true Zimbabwean economic matrix in which different age groups grown and develop on. This implies that other illegal activities are now inseparable from citizens' existence because the prevailing economic conditions completely change the natural disposition of many citizens the young and aged. Nowadays corruption and other illegal activities appears as precocious activities the centre of men's survival. What is important to note is that all these are products of economic status of the nation. Due to long suffering, ceaseless economic hardships, starvation, impoverishment of both rural and urban societies, people instantly look for other alternatives in order to bounce back and earn a living. For the present moment, it is vital not to cast a blame on citizens but rather to blame the prevailing economic conditions. Given that the majority of citizens are living under the poverty datum line, the biggest number of youths are unemployed, indexation is at apex, a directive from planned economy demands taxes in addition to the normal taxation system, what can be done by ordinary citizen, rich and middle class member to earn a living? Without hesitation the citizens instantaneously employ other mechanism to alleviate themselves from unspeakable state of poverty. With this analysis of a nexus between citizen behaviour and economic conditions witnessed in the nation. It is imperative to highlight that, although the issue of legalizing the illegalities appears difficult to be eradicated completely before the attainment of buoyant economy which exist in the blues for a long period of time, balancing act principle is an alternative for the moment. The true panacea to end the illegal behaviour in the nation is to address the economic side and to fix economy calls for stable and genuine politics. If people have food on the table, they tend to relax and focus on the legal channels of survival without any attempt on illegal means. The fact that in Zimbabwe it is difficult if not impossible for an individual to earn a living through the legal way of getting all necessities of life, the alternative mechanism is very dangerous and now its widespread is unstoppable and it reaches all corners of the society. Although it is hideous however, it is worth to unpack the position of individual in the economic ladder of the nation, unfortunately it is a recession ladder, and the way in which the ladder positioned is not simple to change because it is heavily supported by political climbers.

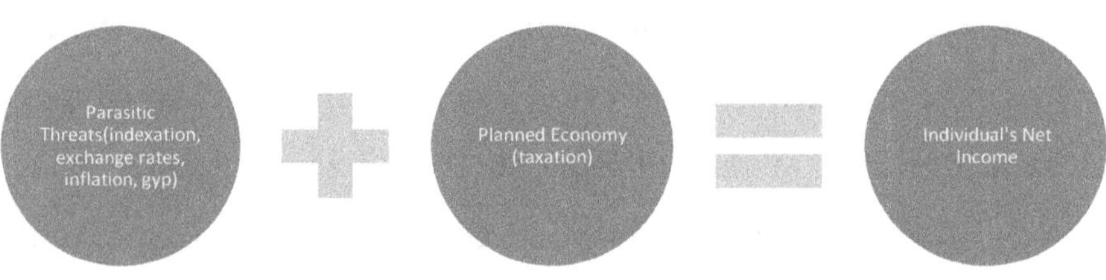

The equation above illustrates the position of an individual in the economic matrix of Zimbabwe. The income per person is subjected to the variety of issues that have an adverse impact for the total income concerned. The income per person is subjected to inflation this heavily affects the wallet of an individual to the extent that citizens would end up possessing wallets with shocking balances that buy nothing. Furthermore, unjustified gyp is a sounding activity of the day this further impoverished the underdeveloped members of the society. Indexation which manifests through the hiking of basic commodities takes a lot from a wallet of an individual. The volatility of exchange rates appears as a sharp jab in the stomach of an individual. All these issues that affect an individual's salary or income can be placed under the umbrella terms to mean parasitic threats. The parasitic threats drain a lot from an individual wallet. In addition, planned economy always keep an eye to the individual's wallet demanding taxes. In response, the planned economy provides some incentives and increments to the individuals, command agriculture is a good example that can be justified under incentives although overemphasis amounts to a matter of justifying the unjustifiable. From another angle, there is a world view an eagle eye to review the way in which people live particularly in terms of the availability of food and poverty reduction. This comes through a choreography route of donations. This channel cannot be exaggerated since it only come in times of need considering the degree of shortages and causes. In addition to that, the donations in most cases meant for the rural people neglecting the urban dwellers who face equivalent predicaments with the rural residents. The issue of scrutiny and rural centred makes one to put a comma in the justification although full stop is yet to be placed. It is important to note that the parasitic threat outweigh the response of the planned economy and the world view aid. As such, the planned economy and external aid fall into knees before the alleviation process of uplifting men from the oasis of recession. Given this picture of economic matrix of the nation, citizens irrevocably legalise the illegalities for them to bounce back and earn a living. In spite of such move Zimbabweans are yet to attain a normal life.

IMPLICATION OF THE PRINCIPLE AT INDIVIDUAL LEVEL

With the mentioned position of individual in the economic matrix, balancing act principle is the answer, a straight way of compromising law and action. The balancing act principle refers to a process in which one tries to please two or more people or groups of people who want different things. At individual level the balancing act principle implies that one is supposed to act in a way of compromising law and action. This automatically avoids gross act of breaching the law at the same time pave way for the survival of an individual.

THE IMPLICATION OF THE PRINCIPLE IN TWO EXTREMES

The balancing act principle is a working solution to address the issue of compartmentalized society. In this case the principle curtail the gross division between the two extremes that is the rise of bureaucracy and the emergence of the extreme poor class. This means that the balancing act principle can be defined as an act of maintaining a delicate balance between two extremes. The mushrooming of a bureaucratic class and its continuous expansion lead to the formation of a compartmentalized society characterized by the rich bureaucracy on the one hand and the extreme poor people on the other hand. Then the balancing act principle is the answer to liquidate the demarcation line between the bureaucracy and extreme poor people. The political leader then required to act in a manner which maintain a delicate balance between two extremes, the diagram below corroborates.

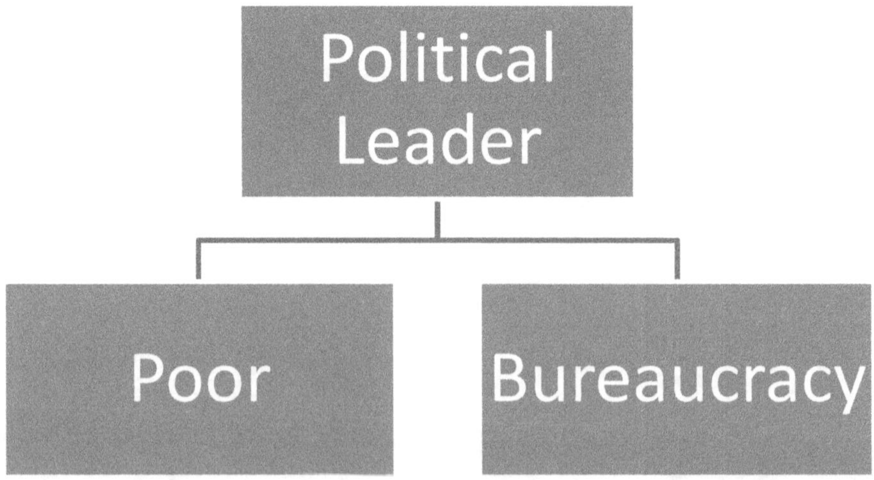

The only way of maintaining a delicate balance is for a political leader to cater for the poor people in order to avoid further impoverishment, in the process alleviating them from the seepage zone of poverty. In the process of keeping an eye to the poor, a political leader should also push for the de-bureaucralization that is reducing the too big bureaucracy. The fall in bureaucracy will create a new trajectory of even distribution of national resources. The even distribution of resources or distribution through equity to achieve functioning equalitarian society is enough to reflect a delicate balance between poor and rich. At this juncture, the balancing act principle can be defined as a process in which a political leader tries to please two or more people or groups of people who want different things. The principle is the way of killing the ills of compartmentalized society. The balancing act principle is a prescription to cure the persecution complex, exhausting the ground of social division and a reinforcing tool for social solidarity. In a compartmentalized society of extreme rich and extreme poor people there is high chances of witnessing the persecution complex. This is through the belief of the poor that the rich individuals one way or the other they will harm them either through their unjustified activities or direct oppression. The balancing act principle through uplifting the status of the poor people makes the persecution complex an erstwhile subject. In a societal level, the balancing act principle is a way of creating irreproachable behaviour which usher in irrepressible living standards, and replaces irreplaceable social solidarity among the Zimbabweans. This is through uniting the rich and poor people, a process which makes the concept of compartmentalized society to be illusion when the rich and poor people live a different life but with the sense of equalitarianism. Although it appears difficult to achieve, but the balancing act principle can liquidates the forces of social division and make them powerless to penetrate into society through even distribution of national resources so that the rich can no longer proceed to be richest at the expense of the others whereas the poor can no longer be impoverished. The incumbent political leaders should be endowed with the spirit of maintaining delicate balance between the rich and poor. This can only be achieved through developing a public spirited feeling and the application of the principle in practical. The implication of political leaders in fighting for the common good for all citizens both rich and poor indeed shows the manifestation of balancing act principle.

IMPLICATION IN MINORITY AND MAJORITY EXTREMES

The issue of compartmentalized society on the basis of rich and poor can be compared to the minority and majority division. A lesson from history is that every polity is made up of two groups of people with diverging and opposing opinions that is to say when a certain dogma, the orthodox opinion prevail the unorthodox can be found. Those who attempt to address this kind of social complexity way back in history ended up follow a stigmatized idea of the good of the majority at the expense of the minority. In Zimbabwean context, the issue of minority and majority division is not a cons cent issue but came into existence hand in hand with the pluralism of political institutions. It is very difficult to end this division because the manifestation of the orthodox view always invites the unorthodox view hence division that establishes the prejudice boundary along the line of minority or majority support and political affiliation. With such irony, what can be done to curtail the extent of division and to prevent polarized society in the zone of majority and minority supports? The answer is the balancing act principle which implies that a political leader should be in a position to maintain a delicate balance between the majority and minority opinions.

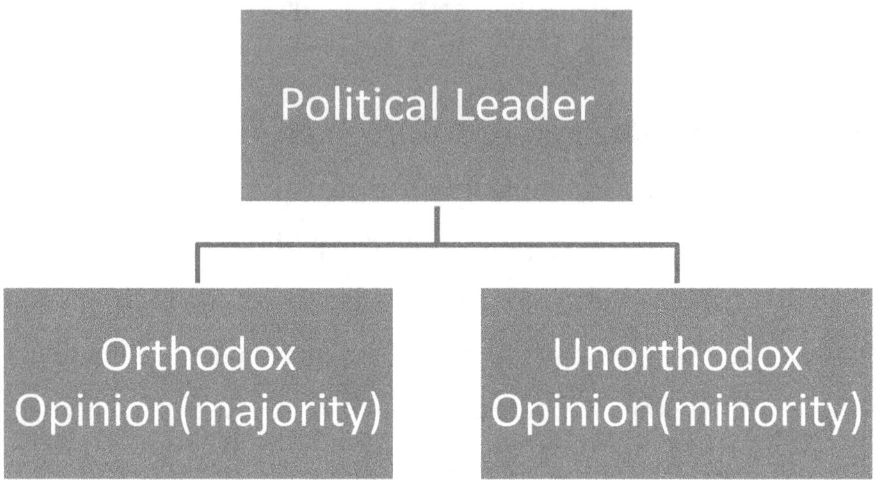

How can an incumbent political leader maintain a delicate balance between two extremes? This question needs to be treated with caution and a minute of accuracy. The modern thinkers who advocate for utilitarianism as a running principle to address the ills of society ended up registering to the profound condemned way of majority good at the expense of the minority. The issue of happiness for the greatest number and arithmetic calculation of utility expose the weakness of the principle. The social contract theorists followed the same condemned road of supporting the majority and always blinking to the minority opinions. In order to maintain a delicate balance between two extremes of majority with orthodox view and minority with unorthodox view, political leader should do what is good for both that is an exact midpoint position to easy the threats of social polarization by avoid penetrating division. He who abandons to do what is good for the people in favor of what they want ended up committing a great error of supporting the majority orthodox view at the expense of the minority opinion. The true panacea to make social division powerless to penetrate deeply into society is to do what is good for the people and not what they want. By doing so, a delicate balance between two extremes can be fully maintained, a clear manifestation of the balancing act principle. Political leaders should be in a position of maintaining a delicate balance between majority and minority extremes in order to cool down polarity and create a solid state. An equipoise of majority and minority extremes liquidates social division and dissipate social polarization due to the eradication of prejudiced boundaries along the line of holding either orthodox or unorthodox view. The ebbing of social polarization is yardstick behind the restoration of genuine politics in Zimbabwe. In addition, the division among citizens along the line of political affiliation is another central issue which calls for the political leaders to take a neutral position and maintain a balance between two extremes of opponents and proponents. The failure to maintain a balance between two opposing opinions in terms of political affiliation creates unprecedented scenario whereby people of the same country divide and produce two distinctive groups with different perception towards each other. This ultimately result in pull and pull or push and push activities rather than pull and push, a solid force that prepared to pull the economic vehicle from recession. Due to the division along political affiliation, every citizen equipped himself or herself with tools to prove one of the political side correct hence, sabotages, unchecked corruption, unscrupulous activities become the order of the day. As it stands now there is no blinking to the fact that, division in terms of political affiliation is a shadow that occlude the political mess as everyone justify his or her stand point with the fundamental freedoms. The way forward is balancing act principle, the political leaders should be in a position to maintain a delicate balance between two extremes of proponents and opponents in politics. The problem with the politics of Zimbabwe is that of creating permanent opponents and permanent proponents. This ossifies the line of divisions an ingredient behind distorted politics. It is good for every citizen to opt for the politics of friendship characterized by cordial relations. The balancing act principle is the answer and workable solution to the situations and challenges that hampering the nation from recording socio-economic development. The act of maintaining a delicate balance between two groups that want different things is a stepping stone towards genuine politics. The principle is critical in reconciling politics with economy that is creating stable politics which act as a breeding ground for buoyant economy. Disunity is a single word that can be used to describe a compartmentalized society, disunity and progress cannot walk together in the same path. Balancing act principle through an act of maintaining balance between two extremes can liquidates the institutionalized structures of social division pave way for social cohesion characterized by invisible social division. The restoration of social cohesion is critical as it facilitates political order which is key for economic development in Zimbabwe. In short, balancing act principle is a necessary tool to restore social order and solidarity and social cohesion is yardstick in shaping the politics of the day and politics is a key determinant for economic position.

CONCLUSION

To sum up concisely, this paper constitutes a working solution to end incessant economic recession, social complexities, and polarization that circumscribe the citizens. The presentation of the correlation of politics and economy reflects economy as a mirror of the goodness and wrongness of politics in an attempt to rebuild the nation. The conceptualization of Zimbabwean politics laid down the fundamental areas that need to be addressed in order to transform the changeable political history to genuine and stable politics that suffice to champion economic development through eradication of economic turbulence. Violence in the form of rampage activities, lack of popular participation, the mushrooming of bureaucracy and its ceaseless expansion are key issues that prevaricate Zimbabwean politics into political upheavals. The repercussions of the mentioned ingredients behind distorted politics continue to reverberate through the economic matrix. The presentation of the correlation of politics and economy is a magic bullet to the economic challenges that strike the nation. The timeframe 2004 to 2018 with a cursory analysis of economic performance suffice to demonstrate how politics correlate with economic meltdown and the proposed way forward is genuine politics. The economic vehicle in most cases was circumscribed by botched political environment which establishes solid boundary in the acceleration path and cause it to zero around poor growth grounds. This paper pays attention to the importance of unity. For Zimbabwe, unity is the workable modus vivendi necessary for development, the practicalities of 2009 to 2013 era justify this line of thinking. Distorted politics always anchored on the way in which elections were conducted. Introduction of political reforms stand as feasible remedy to ceaseless election contestations. The blue prints of distorted politics can be traced phenomenologically from social division that is division along lines of political affiliation, extreme rich and extreme poor, as well as opinions that is either orthodox or unorthodox. The balancing act principle which implies that political leader should be in a position to maintain balance between two extremes is the answer to social ramification. The call for political stability is sine-qua-non for the economic recovery and transformation. In a society with social unrest, trepidation, perplexity, and economic meltdown, stable politics is a panacea to restore social and economic order.

REFERENCE LIST

Acemoglu, D and Robinson, J. A. 2012. *Origin of Poverty*, London: Profile Books Ltd.

Adams, I and Dayson, W. 2003. *Fifty Major Political Thinkers*, London: Routledge.

Apter, D. E. 1997. *The Legitimization of Violence*, London: Macmillan Press.

Bratton, M and Rothchild, D. 1992. *The Institutional Bases of Governance in Africa*, London: Lynne Rienner Publishers.

Lenin, V. 1979. *On Participation of People on Government*, Moscow: Moscow Progress Publishers.

Masunungure, E. 2009. *Defying Winds of Change*, Harare: SAPES.

Mugge, D. 2016. *Journal of European Public Policy*.

Nau, H. R. 2012. *Perspectives on International Relations*, London: SAGE Publishers.

Schumpeter, J. 1976. *Capitalism, Socialism and Democracy,* London: George Allen and Unwin Publishers.

THE CORRELATION

ABOUT THE AUTHOR

An undergraduate student of political science at the University of Zimbabwe matriculated in 2018.